Imani's Library Book

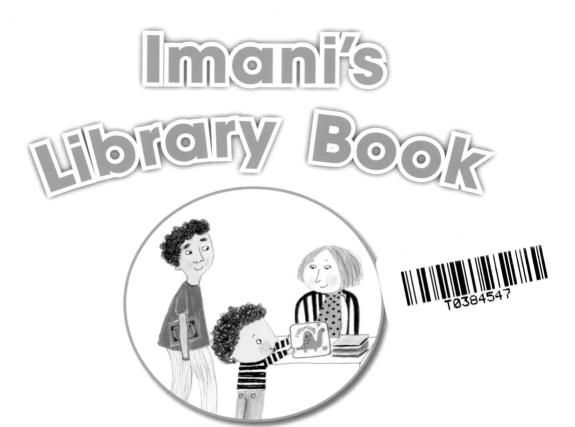

by Alison Hawes
illustrated by Ailie Busby

 CAMBRIDGE
UNIVERSITY PRESS

 UCL
Institute of Education

Imani has a book about dinosaurs.

He takes it back to the library.

Imani looks at a book about birds

but he puts it back.

Imani looks at a book about cars

but he puts it back.

Imani looks at a book about tigers

but he puts it back.

Imani looks at a book about trains

but he puts it back.

Imani looks at the book about dinosaurs.

He takes it home ... again!

Imani's Library Book ✦ Alison Hawes

Teaching notes written by Sue Bodman and Glen Franklin

Using this book

Developing reading comprehension

Imani loves the book about dinosaurs so much that he takes it home again. A small number of sentence structures are used to tell this very recognisable situation. The main body of the story uses a very long sentence with two simple clauses linked by 'but'. This is a challenge at Red band since it requires the reader to coordinate one-to-one correspondence throughout two sentence structures presented in one long line of text. The goal at this band is for the children to follow the print with their eyes, only rarely using finger-pointing at points of difficulty.

Grammar and sentence structure

- One long sentence consolidates one-to-one correspondence
- Punctuation (full stop, use of ellipsis and exclamation marks) supports phrased and expressive reading.

Word meaning and spelling

- Opportunity to rehearse and read a wide range of known high frequency words.
- Practise and consolidation of reading regular decodable words.

Curriculum links

Maths – Information about how many books the children have read and on what topics could be gathered over a week in school and presented in tally charts and graphs.

Language development – Visit the school library and explore how the system works. After each child has chosen a book to borrow, create a short time slot each day where children can recommend what they have read to other children.

Learning outcomes

Children can:

- use punctuation to inform phrasing and expression
- use phonic knowledge to solve new and novel words
- comment on the events and characters in the story, making links to other stories.

A guided reading lesson

Book Introduction

Give each child a book and read the title to them.

Orientation

Give a brief overview of the book, using the verb in the same form as it is in text. Say: *Imani is going to the library. Here is Imani's name* (Put your finger under the word). *He is going to take his book back. What is his book about? Yes, it's a book about dinosaurs. I wonder what sort of book he will take out next.*

Preparation

Page 2: Check that the children know what a library is and that books can be borrowed, but have to be returned within a given time frame. Say: *Imani is carrying his library book. Do you think he likes it? Yes, he's looking at it as they walk to the library.* Draw attention to the book under Dad's arm – he is taking a book back to the library too.

Page 3: Say: *Imani takes it back to the library. Find the word 'library'. Think about the letter you expect to see at the beginning. Yes, /l/.*

Page 4: Rehearse the sentence *'Imani looks at a book about birds but he puts it back.'* by reading it aloud and asking the children to follow each word as you read.